ESTATE PLANNING & ADMINISTRATION

FOR

ESTATE AND TRUST

BENEFACTORS AND BENEFICIARIES

By: **Bob Whitman**
Professor of Law
University of Connecticut
School of Law
Hartford, CT 06105
860-570-5250

Published By: **The Graduate Group**
P.O. Box 370351
West Hartford, CT 06137-0351

ABOUT THE AUTHOR

Bob Whitman is a law professor at the University of Connecticut School of Law, in Hartford, CT, where he teaches courses in trusts and estates and estate planning.

Professor Whitman is the Chair of The Law Professor Advisory Group For Trusts and Estates. He is an Academic Fellow of The American College of Trusts and Estates Counsel; a member of The Real Property, Probate & Trust Law Section of The American Bar Association, The American Law Institute and The Society For Trust and Estates Practitioners. He is a Special Advisor to The Joint Editorial Board of The Uniform Probate Code and a Connecticut Commissioner to The National Conference of Commissioners on Uniform State Laws.

Professor Whitman's career as a teacher and practitioner in the trust and estates field spans some forty years. He has always shown special concern for the need to make this area of the law more understandable to the lay public. He lectures nationally on estate planning and estate administration subjects. He has authored many articles and several books in the field. Professor Whitman is a member of the Bars of Connecticut and New York. He lives in West Hartford, CT, with his wife, Edith, and his family, to whom this book is dedicated.

PREFACE

The purpose of this book is not to attempt to make readers expert in the estate planning and administration field.

Rather, it is the author's goal to help individuals grasp a basic sense of the dynamics of the field, thereby allowing the reader to understand how best to proceed to effectively deal with his or her particular situation.

The author hopes that by presenting a simplified overview of the field he will help his readers to take steps to properly estate plan and, in doing so, to avoid some of the most obvious pitfalls that can prevent a smooth gratuitous transfer of property during life and at death. In particular, the author in this book is attempting to "tool up" the reader, so that intelligent questions can be raised with the professionals retained to assist in estate planning and estate administration.

Armed with the information found in this book, the reader should find it easier to interact with professional advisers.

A well informed and prepared client should get the best service at a reasonable cost and gain the best results from the professionals who are asked to serve.

Thus, it is hoped that this book will be used to allow the reader to gain good estate planning and administration results at a fair price. When carried out with common sense, estate planning and administration can be a most productive experience. If this book will help to achieve that result for the reader, it will have served its purpose well.

DISCLAIMER

The following material is designed to present a general discussion of basic principles of estate planning and estate administration.

This material should not be read as "legal advice," which, when needed, should be obtained by the reader from an attorney of his or her choosing.

TABLE OF CONTENTS

TABLE OF CONTENTS (Cont'd)

CHAPTER 1

SEEING THE BIG PICTURE

There is a bumper sticker that says, "Life's a bitch - and then you die."

In this book, we will be focusing on the last part of that message. Our goal will be to understand how to minimize the expenses and hassles of passing property onto those we want to have it, both during life and at death.

In our country, thankfully, we are all free to create the plan we want for the gratuitous transfer of our assets during our lives and at our death. We are free to set up the plan and we call the shots. The problem, however, is that we face a very complicated tax and legal system that challenges us to come up with effective plans that, as implemented, will work for us and get us what we want.

This book is set up to help you design and implement a

proper plan for transferring your property during life and at death.

CHAPTER 2

SCOPING OUT YOUR PLAN

Most people do not want to spend a lot of their time and money thinking about and making plans surrounding their death.

While early on, we all come to understand our mortality, we are urged at a young age to turn our focus to the positive side of living. Our society tells us to work toward a goal of being "happy" in life. Usually, we come to believe that this involves ideas such as: finding a life partner we can love, finding work that we are happy with, earning an adequate amount of money to support ourselves and our family, settling into a community we enjoy, having children, raising a family, contributing towards the welfare of our society, and, hopefully, staying healthy and solvent into our old age.

In order to achieve our lifetime goals, we are taught early

on the value of planning. We are made to see the value of acquiring an education, saving money, setting priorities, setting limits on our desire for material comforts and planning for a secure and comfortable old age.

If we are successful in mastering the ability to properly balance and control our lives, we will likely, at death, leave assets that can be distributed as we would like.

Importantly, the lives each one of us lead are unique. Each of us has his or her own story. Often, our lives take surprising twists and turns, i.e., some of us never marry; some of us never have children; some of us divorce; face challenges caused by disabilities; face illness, addiction or old age; go bankrupt; win the lottery, etc.

Similarly, each person who we might want to benefit during life or at death is unique. Some beneficiaries are mature and capable of dealing with financial matters. Others may not have these strengths. Special attention needs to be paid to minors, the disabled and later generations.

Each of us acquires different property during life.

For some of us, our major asset is land; for others it is securities. Some of us earn royalties; some of us operate a small business owned by a corporation, or a partnership or a limited liability company. Some of us are farmers, or oil men; or we own a plane, a boat, or a horse. Creating a plan requires that attention be paid not only to our circumstances and the circumstances of those we want to benefit, but also to the mix of assets we have and whether we want those assets distributed to our beneficiaries outright or in trust.

Accordingly, every mature person needs to spend time focusing on his or her life situation. Every person needs to plan for that time when it will be appropriate to turnover assets to others. The most important thing is to recognize that there are no general rules uniformly applicable to every person. Estate planning is a highly individualized endeavor.

EXERCISE NO. 1

Set down in the space provided below, a broad statement of your wishes with regard to who is to gain your property at your death.

At my death, I want my property to go to:

If this cannot happen (perhaps the person you name predeceases you) my alternate choices are:

NOTE HERE: Special circumstances to be considered in creating an estate plan that fits your needs and the needs of those you wish to benefit.

From time to time, as you proceed through this book, go back and review your stated goals in EXERCISE NO. 1. A clear and simple statement of those goals is one of the most important building blocks to accomplish in planning for the distribution of your assets at your death.

CHAPTER 3

SHOULD I SEEK PROFESSIONAL HELP TO ACCOMPLISH MY GOALS?

Few of us never seek professional help in going about life tasks. If we want to do so, we can all learn to fix our own car, make our own clothes and cut our own hair. Yet, few of us bother to attempt to do it all ourselves. The costs are too great in terms of the time various tasks take, the machinery required and the skills needed to be acquired.

Our society allows us to make our own choices regarding when we want professional help. For many, mowing the lawn is a task for family members; for others it is a task for a hired gardener. As the complexity of the task increases, the likelihood is that we will be more inclined to seek professional help.

Estate planning is a task that can be solely done by the

family; or competent professional help can be found and retained. Few young single college students without significant assets bother to seek professional help in organizing and planning their estates. Unless there are unusual circumstances, a young college student will file a Federal income tax return without visiting an accountant and hold money in a bank account without concern about who will inherit the money in the event of her untimely death. A bank account in the joint name of a young married couple may be adequate for their needs. But to plan against the unlikely event of the death of both young parents, in order to protect minor children, is a far more complex matter.

Young married college students with one or more minor children must be concerned with the possibility of untimely death. If because of a car crash there is the untimely death of both young parents, a thought through estate plan will be very helpful in setting a new life course for the surviving minor orphaned children. Whether life insurance was purchased by the young couple may also have great meaning in the future; if insurance exists, how the beneficiary designation was set up may be as important as the face amount of the insurance policy. If death was a result of a car crash, whether there will be proceeds of a wrongful death action, and, if so, how those proceeds will be distributed will be important. A professional planner can, without great cost, provide the guidance needed.

In this book the question of whether professional help with estate planning will be sought is left as an open question.

Where appropriate, the reader will be made to understand that self help can be employed. For instance, it will be made clear that a person is not prevented from drawing her own will or trust documents. A person named as executor of a will can, without obtaining guidance from a professional, assume full responsibility for administering an estate.

For most of the discussion in the book, however, the assumption is made that as needed professional help will be engaged. Even if that help is used sparingly and judiciously, the foundations for a sensible plan can be put in place for a reasonable cost. If the proper documents are professionally drawn at the planning stage, at the time for estate administration there will be far fewer problems.

Assuming that a competent professional will be employed at the planning stage, the important point made in this book is that it is not enough to simply hire the professional and put yourself completely in her hands. A client who has been geared up to understand, in a general way, what is involved in planning is a client who is likely to be better served. A client who is sensitive to the areas of concern, knows where the pitfalls lie and can sense the need for the client to periodically make the common sense judgment call is a client that will be more satisfied and have a smoother ride through both the planning and administration process. That is the fundamental lesson of this book.

CHAPTER 4

GENERAL CONCERNS FACED
AT THE OUTSET OF PLANNING

Assuming that professional help is to be retained at the planning stage, finding the right planner is an extremely important first step.

Regardless of the size of the estate to be planned, there are matters that need to be faced by every person who sets out to plan their estate. These matters are discussed in this chapter.

A. WHO SHOULD YOU TURN TO FOR PROFESSIONAL HELP?

There are a vast variety of professionals who can be called upon to help you to meet your need to plan your estate. Some understanding of the roles each professional can play, some understanding of the concept of the unauthorized practice of law and some understanding of the concept of the "estate planning team" will help to guide you along in the exercise of your judgment as to when and where you wish to seek professional help.

B. PROFESSIONALS WHO MAY PLAY A ROLE IN PLANNING ESTATES

1. The Attorney

The attorney plays a unique role in the estate planning process. Based on state statutes regulating the"practice of law", only an attorney can represent you for the purpose of providing "legal advice" and only an attorney can "practice law."

a. Doing Your Own Drafting

To be absolutely clear on this matter, it is important for you to understand that you are allowed to draw your own legal documents. You will not be forced to retain an attorney to draft your own instruments. Perhaps with the help of an advice book, or a computer program, you may decide that you may want to draw your own will. This is perfectly legal. But, a nonlawyer cannot charge you to do this. Only an attorney can "practice law" and drawing a will constitutes "the practice of law." The terms "legal advice" and "practice of law" are far from crystal clear. What is certain at this point is that only an independent attorney can draft some of the more important legal documents to be created in estate planning. Specifically, only an attorney can represent you in drafting for you a will or a trust.

b. <u>Choosing An Attorney</u>

Not all attorneys are fully familiar with estate planning. Some attorneys are general practitioners, ready to take on any legal problem that comes in their office door.For simple wills and basic estate planning, a general practitioner may be clearly competent. Perhaps more important than the depth of your attorney's knowledge is the question of whether you can develop a good personal relationship with the attorney.The attorney may have proven in other matters to be truly caring, wise in terms of helpful advice and fair in terms of charges. Let common sense and your own sense of your needs be your guide.

It is perfectly appropriate for you to "shop" for your attorney. Most attorneys will offer an initial consultation without charge. During that time, search for details regarding experience and interest in the estate planning field. An attorney who specializes in litigation and who goes to court every day is not likely to be a good choice for estate planning.

The chances are that if you have an initial consultation with three or four attorneys, you will be able to properly judge who is right for you. In the initial interview, be sure to ask the right questions. Learn the basis on which the attorney charges; probe the extent of experience and interest he/she has in the estates field; judge the presence or absence of good chemistry between you and this person.

In choosing a professional who will help you to plan your estate, consider carefully recommendations made to you by friends and other professionals. While it is not a hard and fast rule, an attorney who is a member of a large law firm, or a firm that practices in limited areas, will be more likely to devote substantial time to one area of practice. Generally, an attorney with an advanced degree (e.g., an LL.M. in taxation or estate planning) will have a greater depth of understanding. Generally, an attorney who belongs to an organization which has invited the attorney to membership (e.g., The American College of Trusts and Estates Counsel) will have a more extensive background in the field.

c. The Objectivity of Your Attorney

Unlike some other professionals (e.g., insurance salespersons or stockbrokers) the attorney is not attempting to sell you any product. If the attorney is pressuring you to name the attorney as a fiduciary of your will or your trust, with the idea that a substantial fee can be assured for the attorney at the administration stage, you may wish to find another attorney.

d. The Key Is Retaining Power

The most important idea in this area is that you are in control. So long as you keep control within your family of the "fiduciary positions" created in your will and trust, you and those you have named, can hire the attorney, and, if unsatisfied, fire the attorney.

THIS BEARS REPEATING - The person who is the "fiduciary" is in charge of administration. The fiduciary can hire the attorney, and, if unsatisfied, fire the attorney.

The term "fiduciary" will be used frequently in these materials. A fiduciary is a person, or a corporation, who is to serve in a position of trust (e.g., an executor of a will, a trustee of a trust, a guardian or conservator of the person and/or property of a minor or an incapable person). In your instrument you are able to nominate your fiduciaries. We will discuss this matter further in CHAPTER 14.

2. Accountants

An accountant is often the professional who may at tax time call attention to the need for you to engage in estate planning. Many accountants have familiarity with estate planning and can be extremely helpful. But, remember that an accountant cannot represent you to draw your will or trust, or appear in a court of law in order to represent you. Even if an accountant works for a large accounting firm with an estate planning department, (and the accountant is a lawyer admitted to practice in your state) if you have come to the accounting firm seeking estate planning advice, the accounting firm can offer to you specialists who are available to discuss your estate planning needs and prepare for you a document outlining a suggested estate plan, but they cannot draw the needed legal documents. For those documents, you must bring the suggested estate plan to your estate planning attorney.

There are dual practitioners — persons who are trained in both accounting and law — who hold themselves out as engaged in the practice of both accounting and law. As your attorney, that person can draft your will or trust.

Ideally, if your accountant created an elaborate estate plan for you, it will be approved by your drafting attorney. Much time and trouble can be saved by introducing the accountant and the drafting attorney early on, so that at an early stage they can come to some joint recommendations regarding what they propose to you by way of a plan.

3. Bankers

Bank trust departments may actively seek to assist you in developing an estate plan. This may be particularly true if you have a substantial estate and keep substantial funds on deposit with the bank.

Unlike the conservatism that exists in connection with attorney and accounting advertisements, the trust department of a bank chartered to administer estates and trusts (a corporate fiduciary) will likely actively market its services. It will also often stress to you the advantages of deciding to name a corporate fiduciary as your executor and/or your trustee. It may actively seek to have you appoint the bank as a fiduciary, whereas the attorney and accountant will be more likely to let you come to the conclusion that you want them to serve.

Again, a corporate fiduciary cannot actually draw a will or trust. Instead, the bank will suggest that you contact your own attorney. If you indicate that you do not have your own attorney, the bank will provide a list of law firms that you may choose to call. Not surprisingly, those firms may have strong connections with the bank and may support the bank's suggestion that you name the bank as your fiduciary. By long standing custom, if the bank is named the fiduciary in the will, unless there are extraordinary circumstances at the death of the maker of the will (the testator), the bank will name the attorney who drafted the will to represent the bank in the administration of the estate.

4. Financial Planners

Financial planners, including for this discussion insurance salespersons and stockbrokers, may also be helpful in suggesting the need for estate planning. These individuals may also be able to recommend an attorney, if you do not have one in mind. An attorney recommended by a financial planner might have a strong bent towards recommending planning that would be helpful to the individual who recommends him.

It is important to remember that someone who sells insurance may always view insurance as an important part of any estate plan. It may also be the case that an attorney that is recommended by an insurance agent may have strong ties to the insurance agent and may tend to confirm a suggestion that more insurance be an important part of the estate plan. In general, it is always important to gauge whether the advice being given to you by any planner is tempered by the position of the party offering the advice.

5. The Estate Planning Team

All of the individuals discussed above, taken together, represent the estate planning team". Ideally, the entire team that may be working on your matter will communicate early on and come to agreement so that you are not getting conflicting recommendations.

C. SEEK INDEPENDENT OBJECTIVE ADVICE

It bears repeating that, of all the members of the team, those individuals (i.e., the attorney and the accountant) who are not directly selling a product, may be able to provide the most objective advice. Where, however, there is a close tie between the attorney and another member of the team selling a service, there may not actually be an opportunity to hear an objective opinion.

Thus, if the attorney is recommended to you by the person selling insurance, it may be asking too much to expect that the attorney will advise you, contradicting the insurance salesperson, that you do not need more insurance. When in doubt, seeking an independent second opinion would be a sensible way to proceed.

CHAPTER 5

UNDERSTANDING THE LAWS
GOVERNING GRATUITOUS TRANSFERS

Prior to dealing further with some of the many complications with which you will need to familiarize yourself with as you formulate and then implement your estate plan, it is important at this point that you have an overview of the law that will impact your effort to properly distribute your estate, both during life and at death.

In order to keep things simple, let us make the following assumptions:

The person reading this chapter is:

1. A citizen of the United States who is an adult of legal age (each state sets its own legal age, but most often it is 18 rather than 21).

2. A domiciliary of one of the fifty states of the United States or the District of Columbia. Your domicile is that place which you consider to be your permanent home and, if away, where you intend to return.

3. A person who has mental capacity to make a will, trust or other legal document; and

4. A person who is capable of exercising his or her own free will.

A. SYSTEMS OF THE LAW

Under our system of law in the United States, laws are created by 1) the federal government, 2) state governments and 3) local authorities.

Courts, both federal and state, also create law by deciding cases, often by looking to and following earlier precedents; courts also decide on the meaning of the statutes passed by authorized law-making authorities.

So, for example, the laws regarding the formalities required to make a will are to be found in the statutes of each of the states. Each state legislature is free to decide on its own requirements for what will constitute a valid will.

Federal transfer taxes for transfers made during life (the federal gift tax) and for transfers at death (the federal estate tax) are passed by Congress and implemented by the Internal Revenue Service (IRS).

Separate transfer tax laws are passed by state legislatures.

Federal law may also set down rules to control various aspects of what may come up when you transfer property (e.g., at your death, federal law will impact the transfer of your property if you are transferring property that is environmentally unsafe).

For the most part, however, it is state law that will control the passage of your property, because, under our Constitution, powers that are not specifically delegated to the federal government are reserved to the states.

B. STATE LAWS

Focusing on state law regarding the transfer of property, in an effort to gain uniformity among the states, an organization - The National Conference of Commissioners On Uniform State Laws - promulgates uniform laws which are then offered to the state legislatures for enactment as state law.

The principal uniform law created in the area of our interest is The Uniform Probate Code (UPC).

The UPC has been adopted in about one third of the states. This will be the state statutory law that we will most often refer to in this book.

EXERCISE 2.

State below, the name of the state in which you reside and which you consider to be your permanent place of residence (your domicile). For purposes of simplicity, we will not discuss the possibility that some persons may, because of unusual circumstances, not be sure of their domicile; or because they spend part of the year in different locations there is a possibility that they will be found by more than one state to be a domiciliary of the state.

The state of my domicile is:

CHAPTER 6

CREATING A LIST OF YOUR
FINANCIAL HOLDINGS

The goal of estate planning is to arrive at a sensible plan for disposing of your assets to those who you want to benefit during life and at death. Various factors, such as taxes, legal rules and costs, will effect the choices you are likely to make.

In order to see the big picture, at the start of your planning you need to categorize and list all of the assets you own and the name or names in which the assets are held.

You also need to set down your income sources, expectations regarding retirement, your present expenses and the expenses you will likely incur in the future. Information on insurance, including health insurance, also is necessary to round out the picture of your financial holdings.

While you are in the process of creating your list of assets, you can also set up a record of important information such as your date of birth, social security number, the location of your safe deposit box, if you have one, the listing of all bank accounts, where you keep your securities, insurance policies and other important documents.

EXERCISE NO. 3.

Refer back to EXERCISE NO. 1, page 6. Create a chart showing in as much detail as possible, a list of your financial holdings. For each asset, be sure to indicate the name(s) in which the asset is held. If you know the tax basis for the asset, be sure to list that as well. (The concept of tax basis for your property will be discussed in CHAPTER 18 infra.)

Create a record of important facts so that if something happens to you, the person who will be taking over for you can more easily deal with your affairs. Be sure to tell several people where your important documents are kept.

CHAPTER 7

HOW YOU HOLD TITLE TO YOUR PROPERTY IS IMPORTANT

There is a titleholder for every piece of property that belongs to you. If you are single, you may hold title to the property you own in your sole name; or you may hold title jointly with a relative or friend.

In this chapter we are going to concentrate on the holding of title by married couples.

There are two basic schemes in the United States with regard to ownership of marital property:

A. SEPARATE PROPERTY

Separate property exists in all of our states except for nine states which adhere to the community property system discussed below. Under the separate property ownership system, which originated in England, if title is in the name of the husband, he owns the property; if title is in the name of the wife, she owns the property. In our later discussions, you will come to see why these concepts are important for estate planing purposes.

To safeguard a spouse against disinheritance in a separate property state, there will be a statute requiring a minimum share for a surviving spouse. Every spouse has this "non-barrable statutory share", unless for some reason (e.g., abandonment) this "non-barrable right" is not provided for by applicable statute, or it has been waived by a premarital or postmarital agreement.To safeguard the rights of a married couple in divorce proceedings, the divorce court can exercise its power of "equitable distribution," allowing the divorce court to divide the couple's assets, regardless of who holds title, in a fair and equitable manner. The court will assert this power unless the parties themselves come to an agreed upon set of terms for dividing property which they will set forth in a separation agreement.

B. COMMUNITY PROPERTY

Community property exists in eight states (Arizona, California, Idaho, Louisiana, Nevada, New Mexico, Texas, Washington). Wisconsin is the ninth community property state and it is the one state to have enacted the Uniform Marital Property Act.

In a community property state, each spouse is the owner of an undivided one-half interest in the community property. The fundamental principal of community property is that all earnings of the spouses and property acquired from earnings during the marriage, are community property. The death of one spouse dissolves the community. The deceased spouse owns and has testamentary power (the power to transfer assets by will) only over his or her one-half community share.

The following illustration should help to clarify the difference between a separate property jurisdiction and a community property jurisdiction.

H works at a job outside the home. H earns $75,000 annually. W is a housewife earning nothing. After 20 years:

1. In a separate property jurisdiction, if H bought various property in his name from savings, H is the owner of all of the property.

2. In a community property jurisdiction, W owns half of all of H's earnings. W, therefore, owns one-half of all the property that has been bought in H's sole name.

Here is some more information about the separate property and community property systems:

1. If H and W live in either a separate property state or a community property state, if they purchase out-of-state realty, because the law of the state in which the realty is

located governs their ownership rights, if the realty is located in a community property state, the property will be held in community; if the realty is located in a separate property state, the person in whose name the title is taken is the owner.

2. In separate property states, title can be taken in the sole name of a party or in his name and the name of one or more persons.

3. Commonly, married couples hold title to their property in both their names, with a right of the survivor to automatically take the entire property at the death of the first spouse to die. The couple will likely be holding the property "in joint name with right of survivorship."

   If they prefer, a married couple can each simply own an undivided one half interest in the property. In that case, the couple will be holding "as tenants in common." In CHAPTER 16 we shall see that how property is held is an important consideration in estate planning.

EXERCISE NO. 4

For all real property owned, list each property, give a description, a value, and the title that the property is held in. To find out exactly how real property is held, check the deed for the property; to find out exactly how securities are held, check stock certificates or ascertain the title to the brokerage account in which the securities are held.

CHAPTER 8

MATTERS OF CONCERN TO EVERY PERSON: FUNERAL ARRANGEMENTS AND ORGAN DONATION

While engaging in estate planning some thought should be given to funeral arrangements and anatomical gifts.

A. FUNERAL ARRANGEMENTS

Funeral arrangements planned in advance help relieve the surviving family of the stress and burden of making last minute arrangements. Unfortunately, some funeral directors will play on the emotions of the bereaved and suggest extraordinarily expensive arrangements on the theory that you can show your love for the deceased by spending lavishly.

In order to head off a financial disaster in connection

with funeral arrangements, some individuals choose to prepay for their funeral - others carefully leave detailed memos indicating what their wishes are, including the wish that inordinate amounts of money not be spent on a funeral. Because a death brings strong emotional reactions, it is important to work to prevent individuals in the funeral business from taking unfair advantage of the situation. Furthermore, it is most helpful for the surviving family to know whether there is a preference for cremation, burial or some other arrangement. If burial is wanted, it is important to arrange for a grave sight while living. Often, several cemetery plots will be wanted so that spouses and children can all be buried alongside each other. Again, making advance arrangements is the key.

B. ANATOMICAL GIFTS

A majority of states require hospital administrators to discuss organ donation with next of kin. There remains a critical shortage of body parts and organs which are needed for transplantation.

The sale or purchase of body parts is prohibited, but agreeing to donation can be easily done. In many jurisdictions, provision is made so that a driver's license will set out an intent to agree to organ donation. In other cases, a simple signed statement indicating a desire at death to allow organ donation will suffice.

Unfortunately, there are not enough persons making

provision for donating their body parts upon their death. Perhaps this is because payment for organ donations is not allowed, or because thinking about the matter is not looked forward to.   Also, religious beliefs may discourage donation. Hopefully, as time goes on and the benefits of organ donation are brought to the attention of the public, needed donations will be made.

CHAPTER 9

THE DURABLE POWERS OF ATTORNEY AND OTHER STRATEGIES FOR DEALING WITH INCAPACITY

Concern for the possibility that a person may lose capacity, but continue to live on and require attention to be paid to his or her financial details, will prompt advance planning to meet this potential concern.

In this chapter, we will consider three planning devices that can be used to deal with the possibility of future incapacity - the durable power of attorney, conservatorship and a revocable living trust.

A. THE DURABLE POWER OF ATTORNEY

If no advance arrangement is made, upon loss of capacity an interested person may seek court appointment as the conservator of the person and/or property of the incapable in order to manage the assets of a person who has lost capacity under court supervision. (Conservatorship is discussed at B. below).

A less complicated planning device than relying on conservatorship is the execution, while capable, of a durable power of attorney. A number of states have adopted the Durable Power of Attorney Act, which also appears in the Uniform Probate Code (UPC).

A power of attorney allows a capable person to appoint a person (the holder of the power) as the agent for the person creating the power (the power giver) and to indicate in the document the scope of the powerholders authority.

At common law, the authority given in a power of attorney lapses upon the principal's (the power giver's) loss of capacity. At loss of capacity the agent (the power holder) could no longer act on the principal's behalf. If a state statute authorizes the creation of a durable power of attorney, execution of an effective durable power of attorney will solve this problem. Under a durable power of attorney, the agent is able to continue to act in spite of the fact that the creator of the power has lost capacity.

Durable powers of attorney need to be drawn with some care. There is concern that the holder of the power might misuse the power. Thus, in some cases, the power will be drawn so that it will not take effect until the actual loss of capacity of the principal. A method of determining loss of capacity can be written into the document. In other cases, physical possession of the power will be withheld from the agent while the principal has capacity. This will prevent the improper use of the power by the agent while the principal has capacity. Durable powers of attorney can also present problems when the power is to be used by the agent. Third parties, concerned with their own liability, may be reluctant to transact business with an agent authorized under a durable power of attorney. If the power is in some way not proper on its face, collateral evidence of the agent's authority may be called for, or if the principal still has capacity, the consent of the principal to the use of the power may be asked for. Third parties may be particularly concerned about relying on a power if the power was executed a long time before the attempt to exercise it. Reexecution of powers every couple of years can help prevent a claim of staleness.

One way to avoid the potential problem of the power holder being unable to convince a third party to honor a power of attorney is to allow the holder of a power to also become a direct signatory on a bank account, or similar document evidencing title to property (e.g., a brokerage account).

If the agent is given direct authority for withdrawal from a bank account, care should be taken to spell out to the bank exactly the intent of the principal. On a bank account, for example, the question of ownership of the account at death should be made clear at the time the account is opened. If the agent's authority to withdraw funds is only for the "convenience" of the principal who cannot easily get to the bank, this limited purpose should be made clear. Otherwise, there may be a claim at the death of the owner of the bank account that the agent was intended to become the owner of the account. Awareness of this potential problem will help to clarify the nature of the holding at the time the bank account is opened.

If interested parties feel at any time that an infirm person is being abused or taken advantage of by any person (including a person who is a signatory on a bank account, or who holds authority under a durable power of attorney, or who holds authority as conservator, or as the trustee of a trust) then the proper authorities must be notified and steps taken to assure that the infirm person is not being taken advantage of.

On the other hand, it is important to recognize that persons who have capacity and the ability to handle their financial affairs may late in life make decisions that their family may not approve of (e.g., ninety year old announcing plans to marry younger person). Clearly under our law, until a person loses capacity, the person is entitled to make decisions that suit that person in spite of the fact that these decisions may anger family members who have preconceived ideas as to how the infirm person should act, and should not act, before death.

B. CONSERVATORSHIP

Every state will have statutory authority for the appointment of a conservator (sometimes called a guardian) to see to the needs of an incapable person. In some states, the statutes will allow a capable person to nominate a conservator, in the event that the person loses capacity and an interested party seeks the appointment of a conservator of the person and/or the property of a conservator.

Conservatorship is a more formal relationship than holding power under a durable power of attorney. A conservator is appointed by an appropriate court upon the application of an interested person who claims that the person in need of assistance (the ward) cannot manage his or her financial affairs. The conservator, upon appointment, is directly responsible to the court for proper stewardship and the applicable statute is likely to set out formal periodic accounting requirements that require the conservator to account to the court.

Often, because of the expense involved in having to account to the court, the parties may prefer to work with a durable power of attorney. But if there is concern by an interested party that the holder of a durable power is not acting in the best interests of the creator of the power, an application for the appointment of a conservator may be filed with the court. If the court does appoint a conservator of the property of the ward, the holder of the durable power of attorney must turn over the assets she holds to the conservator and account for her stewardship.

Knowledgeable professionals may often advise clients to plan in a manner that will avoid mandatory formal accountings. The reason for this is the expenses that accompany such formal accounting. In a formal accounting proceeding, the individual accounting may wish to be represented by counsel, whose fees will be paid from the assets being accounted for. Minors and contingent interests, including the interests of unknown or unascertained individuals, may also need to be represented by a guardian ad litem (a guardian for the one proceeding only as opposed to a guardian of the person and/or property of a person who would be serving on a continuous basis). While all of these individuals are needed in order, in legal theory, to protect the interests of the parties affected by the proceeding in court, these costs, taken from the fund being accounted for, can substantially reduce the value of the fund, or completely exhaust the fund.

Accordingly, planning is often done to avoid the need for formal in court proceedings. Where the durable power of attorney is considered too informal and conservatorship is considered too inflexible and costly, if sufficient assets are involved the planner may recommend the use of a revocable living trust. The advantages of a revocable living trust in administering the property of a person who may be aging and concerned about becoming incapable are considerable.

C. REVOCABLE LIVING TRUST

In order to gain an understanding of the advantages of a revocable living trust, whether it is funded or unfunded, it is appropriate to first define and explain the trust concept.

Generally, if we say a person "owns" an asset, we mean that the asset is in the person's sole name and that the person has complete control over the asset. The owner has complete title to the asset. At common law, a need developed to establish a form of ownership which divided legal and equitable ownership of assets.

Where, for example, a nobleman planned to leave to join a crusade, the nobleman would have a concern for the possibility that he might not return from the crusade (e.g., he might be killed or captured, taken prisoner and held for ransom). If that were to happen, who would look after his land holdings and his other wealth? Perhaps he was leaving minor children behind, or a wife who was not considered capable of dealing with the supervision and protection of his property. By this time, the common law developed and had established two distinct ownership rights to property: 1) There was the "legal title," which was held by a person who had title that could be asserted in the courts of law and 2) there was also the possibility that other persons could hold the "equitable title," which could be asserted in the courts of equity. To better understand this concept, it is important to realize that, depending on the action to be brought, a person seeking redress from a court had to bring his action to the proper court (i.e., law court or court of equity).

Thus, if X created a document that gave legal title to his assets to Y, as trustee, to hold the assets under the terms of a trust document for the benefit of Z, X was the creator of the trust, Y was the trustee who held the legal title to the assets, as trustee, under the terms of the trust document for the benefit of Z. If necessary, Z could enforce his right to be benefited from the trust in a court of equity. Y, as trustee for Z's benefit, owed Z fiduciary duties and was required to serve Z in accordance with the terms of the trust.

If, under the terms of the document (the trust instrument) X gave up the right to later change the document, the trust created by the terms of the document is called: an irrevocable trust. If under the terms of the trust instrument X retained the right to later revoke the trust, the trust is called: revocable. If the trust is set up in X's will, the trust is called a testamentary trust and the trust does not become active until X's death. If the trust is set up by a document by X during X's life, the trust is called: a living trust. A living trust can be established by the creator declaring the trust (a declaration of trust) or by an agreement with the trustee (an agreement of trust).

Therefore, if X wishes to plan for an orderly transfer of the administration of his assets in the event of his incapacity, he may decide to solve this problem by using a revocable trust which will be established by a separate trust document created by X during his life - a living revocable trust.

In creating the trust, X can provide that he, X, shall be the trustee of the trust during his life. X can retain the right to revoke the trust at any time, so long as X retains the capacity to do this. X can fund the trust with his assets and retain all of the income earned by the assets of the trust during his life. X can transfer to her revocable living trust all of the assets which she wants to place in the trust during her life. Because X still retains complete control over the trust assets (she can revoke the trust and take back the assets at any time) there are no federal gift tax consequences on the transfer of property into the trust, there are no federal income tax consequences in connection with the income earned by the assets of the trust (X retains the right to receive all of the income during her life) and since X retains full control of the assets during her life, the assets will remain in X's estate at his death for purposes of the federal estate tax.

The purpose of creating the living revocable trust is not to attempt to engage in tax planning. If a change in tax consequences is wanted, the trust will be drawn as an "irrevocable trust," rather than as a "revocable trust".

Assets held in the sole name of a decedent need to be dealt with by a court of probate in order to clear the title to the assets so that they can be distributed to the beneficiaries of the probate estate. One purpose behind creating and funding (transferring assets into) the trust would be to avoid probate by creating non-probate assets that can pass under the terms of the trust to the person to be benefited at X's death. In this way, planning for future events, including the death of both parents leaving minor children, can be accomplished without the need to have probate of the assets that were put into the trust before death.

Another important advantage of creating and funding a revocable living trust during life is that the trust can set up a plan for administering the trust assets in the event of the incapacity of the creator of the trust.

The trust can provide that in the event that the trust creator loses capacity, a named successor trustee can take over the administration of the trust. The terms of the trust can establish a procedure for determining when the creator of the trust has lost capacity. For instance, it may require one or more physicians to declare that the trust creator has lost capacity. The trust may also set out a series of objective criteria for establishing capacity.

If the creator of the trust is serving as the trustee of the trust, at the point when the trust creator dies or loses capacity, a named successor trustee can serve as trustee. The successor trustee can be an individual, or a corporate fiduciary. Provisions can be made for co-trustees if desired. There can also be provision for waiving the need to post a bond or for providing formal accountings. The powers of the trustee can be set forth in the trust instrument, as well as provisions for dealing with many other matters that may concern the trustee. Detailed provisions for distributing the trust property on the death of the trustee can be provided for.

All of the property placed in the trust passes by the terms of the trust; there is no need to clear title to trust assets and probate is avoided for the trust assets.

With so many potential advantages, why would individuals use a durable power of attorney or rely on the appointment of a conservator, when and if needed? First, there is often a lack of awareness of the problems that can be caused by incapacity. Many of us simply are caught up in the immediate problems of day-to-day living. We have no time or inclination to consider the future and the difficulties that incapacity could cause. Next, establishing a living trust involves finding a capable attorney. There will be an expense involved in having the trust drawn. There will be more expenses in having assets transferred into the trust. For instance, if realty is to be placed into the trust during the life of the trust's creator, a new deed transferring the property to the trust will have to be drawn. Unexpectedly, if the realty is transferred into the trust, on a decision to refinance a mortgage, the property owner may find that the terms of the original mortgage prohibited placing the property into a trust and the bank will refuse to refinance the mortgage until the property is taken out of the trust and returned to the sole name of the property owner. Underlying this unwillingness to accept transfer of the realty into trust during the life of the owner may be law in the jurisdiction that gives more rights to creditors against property held in sole name than to property held in trust.

On balance, therefore, for younger persons, a revocable living trust may be set up for estate planning purposes. Upon the death of the individual, her will can provide for a "pour over" which will direct the executor to pay over the residuary estate from the will to the trustee of the living trust so that those assets will be held and distributed in accordance with the terms of the trust.

For younger persons, the planner may not encourage an immediate transfer of assets into the trust. In that case, the living trust will be unfunded and may remain so until the death of the trust creator. Then, other assets, such as retirement funds and insurance funds can be distributed to the living trust in the event both parents die. In such a case, the living trust, whether funded during life, or not, is used to consolidate the assets of the estate without the need for probate of all of the assets. When this happens, the planner will explain to the client that the revocable living trust being created will not be immediately used to deal with concerns about incapacity.

Instead, until the trust is to be funded with the trust creator's assets, a durable power of attorney will be used to authorize the holder of the power to administer the assets of the creator of the power in the event of her loss of capacity.

CHAPTER 10

HEALTH CARE POWERS AND LIVING WILLS

A. HEALTH CARE POWERS

A health care power may be included in a durable power of attorney, or, it may be created as a separate document.The health care agent can be given authority to decide proper medical treatment for a patient who no longer has capacity, e.g., whether the patient should be placed on a life support system; when a life sustaining system should be withdrawn. A health care power can be held by the creator of the family, or by the holder of the power, and, if desired, a copy of the power can be given to the creator's primary physician.

B. LIVING WILLS

A living will can be executed to show the intent of the person who is executing the power with regard to the extent that the person wants "extraordinary measures" taken to prolong life. Living wills, for instance, will allow a person to declare that if he is terminally ill, and he loses consciousness, he wishes to have withheld from him nutrition and hydration, if there is no reasonable expectation that he will regain consciousness. Living wills are state statute-based and must conform to specific requirements which are announced in each states statute. Forms for living wills and execution instructions can often be found in a legal stationery store.

For any of the documents that we are considering, it is most important that attention be paid to the requirements for execution needed to validate the document. This important point is emphasized in the next chapter.

CHAPTER 11

EXECUTION FORMALITIES

At this point, we have already learned about a considerable number of documents that can be drawn in order to facilitate the estate planning process.

These documents are often drawn to meet the requirements of state statutes. The statute authorizing the use of the document may also establish execution formalities that are required in order to cause the document to be valid. For example, in many states for a will to be valid, it may require witnessing by two witnesses; a trust that is to transfer realty may require a writing and witnessing. If a copy of the trust is to be placed on the land records, notarization may be required.

One clear advantage of retaining the services of a capable professional is that she will understand the execution procedures and formalities required for each document. For example, she will explain that whereas there is only to be one original copy of your will (so that there is no ambiguity regarding whether you later intended to revoke it when you ripped up the original copy) there can be a number of original copies of your living revocable trust.

Having a number of copies of a living revocable trust may prove useful because the authority of the trustee is evidenced by the terms of the trust and third parties in dealing with the trustee may want to be able to retain an original copy of the trust instrument.

If, on balance, a decision is made to prepare the documents needed to implement an estate plan without retaining the services of an attorney, careful attention must be paid to the execution formalities required to validate the various documents. A stationery store may be able to supply you with computer software for the various forms of documents we are discussing or they may have printed forms. If the decision is made to execute forms without the assistance of an attorney, then careful attention must be given not only to filling out the forms, but also to the instructions provided for the execution of the documents. The law is often unforgiving where the exact execution requirements are not followed.

CHAPTER 12

ESTATES THAT PASS AT DEATH WITHOUT CONCERN FOR THE FEDERAL ESTATE TAX

Under the Federal gift and estate tax, every person has one unified credit towards taxable gifts made during life and the final gifts that are to be made at death. Under present law, based on the allowable credit available to each person, by the year 2006 every person will be able to pass up to one million dollars of property (either taxable because of a taxable lifetime gift, or because of a taxable transfer at death) without being subjected to the Federal gift and estate tax system.

The actual amount of the unified credit shelters an amount of property referred to as the "exemption equivalent". For example, when the unified credit was $92,800, the exemption equivalent was $600,000. ($600,000 of taxable property created a tax of $92,800 which the unified credit covered).

Thus, prior to 1997, if none of the available unified credit was used, every person could transfer $600,000 without incurring tax.

From 1997 until 2006, the unified credit, and corresponding exemption equivalent is increasing, as shown by the table below, so that as shown in the following table, in 2006, and thereafter, the exemption equivalent will be $1 million.

Year	Amount of Exemption Equivalent
1998	$ 625,000
1999	$ 650,000
2000 and 2001	$ 675,000
2002 and 2003	$ 700,000
2004	$ 850,000
2005	$ 950,000
2006	$1,000,000

The 1997 Act also contains a number of other changes.

Most important to our basic understanding of tax planning is the indexing of the $10,000 annual gift tax exclusion discussed in CHAPTER 18 and the $1 million GST exemption discussed in CHAPTER 21

If a person has significant assets so that it is expected that he or she will be subject to the Federal transfer tax system, there is one unitary tax table with graduated tax rates that will be applied for gifts and estate transfers that are to be taxed.

Before any tax becomes due, each person is able to use up his or her entire allowable unified credit. After the allowable unified credit is exhausted, then the progressive tax rate is applied to the taxable gifts and estate transfers which a person has made during his or her life and then at death. When it applies, the applicable tax rates for the Federal gift and estate tax are quite substantial. Starting at the 37% bracket, transfer taxes can reach an effective tax top rate of 60%.

In addition to the Federal gift and estate tax, there is also a separate tax for generation-skipping trusts, which will be discussed later in CHAPTER 20.

It is most important to understand that Federal gift and estate taxes and the generation-skipping transfer tax are taxes that come on top of the Federal income tax. Thus, persons who accumulate large estates clearly have a need for tax-driven estate plans. These plans are discussed in CHAPTER 16.

For now, it is enough to say that married couples whose total joint assets are less than the available amount covered by their allowable unified credits can engage in relatively simple non-tax driven estate planning. Simple non-tax driven estate plans are discussed in CHAPTER 14.

EXAMPLE:

By 2006, Husband (H) and Wife (W) will each have an exemption equivalent of $1 million dollars. If H and W's combined assets are well below $1 million dollars, and if they have made no taxable lifetime gifts and they each hold half of the assets, having simple wills leaving all assets to each other will not subject their estates to the Federal estate tax.

EXERCISE NO. 5

Total the entire value of the assets in your estate (and the estate of your spouse if you are married). If the amount is less than the available "exemption equivalent," you are able to avoid engaging in tax-driven estate planning.

CHAPTER 13

SIMPLE NON-TAX DRIVEN ESTATE PLANNING

Smaller estates that are not subject to the Federal gift and estate tax can be planned for without the need to deal with the complexity of tax-driven instruments.

A. INTRODUCTION

Suppose we consider H and W, a young married couple without substantial estates. Commonly, H and W will hold the bulk of their assets in joint name. The most common form of joint name holding is joint name, with right of survivorship. (In some jurisdictions married couples can also hold jointly by the entireties, but this less common joint holding will not be discussed). Ownership of jointly held assets pass to the survivor on the death of the first person to die. If preferred, the named couple can hold property in joint tenancy. In joint tenancy, on the death of the first to die, his interest will pass because of the nature of the holding to the surviving joint tenant. If the holding is in tenancy in common, on the death of one party, his share of the property will then be passed to his estate. That will mean that the property will pass by his will, or, if no will, by the terms of the intestacy statute.

If property is to be held jointly, the bank accounts (both savings and checking) will likely be held in joint name, with right of survivorship. The house, if they own one, will likely be purchased in joint name and their investments will likely be held in joint name.

Retirement funds will be held in the name of each of the spouses who has made some provision for retirement. By Federal law, on the death of the first spouse to die, any available retirement funds will pass to the surviving spouse. A signed waiver by a spouse would be needed to alter this result. Insurance will have a beneficiary designation permitting the surviving spouse to be designated as the primary beneficiary. In an unusual case, someone other than a surviving spouse might be named as the primary beneficiary.

If there is a safety deposit box, it will likely be held in joint names, so that on the death of one of the spouses, the survivor will be able to gain easy access to the box.

B. PROPERTY HELD IN JOINT NAME WITH RIGHT OF SURVIVORSHIP

Property held in joint name with right of survivorship is by far the most common form of property ownership in the United States. One advantage of this holding is that it avoids the need for probate of the jointly held assets at the death of the first of the joint tenants to die. This is because at the first death, the property will automatically pass to the surviving joint owner without the need to clear title to the asset. Property that passes automatically by the nature of the holding on the death of the party is referred to as "non-probate property".

If, on the other hand, property is held in the sole name of a person and the person dies, that property is referred to as "probate property". Probate property will not be able to automatically pass at death because of the nature of holding. The property will be subject to probate.

Therefore, the two major divisions of property holding for estate planning purposes are: non-probate property and probate property.

C. NON-PROBATE PROPERTY

This is property that will pass at death because of the nature of the holding. Non-probate property will include property that is held in joint name, property that will pass by a beneficiary designation (e.g., an insurance policy which designates a third party as beneficiary, a retirement fund that designates a third party as a beneficiary; property held in a living revocable trust which is to be distributed to named third parties on the death of the creator of the trust).

D. PROBATE PROPERTY

This is property that will be subject to probate. The purpose of probate will be to clear title to the probate assets and see to their distribution to those persons who are entitled to the property at the death of the property owner.

If X during life holds property in his own name, then at X's death, if he leaves a valid will, the property will pass through probate and be distributed to those persons who are entitled to take under the will.

In his will, X will likely nominate someone (it may be an individual, or a corporate fiduciary, or more than one person) to be the executor of his will. The executor is also broadly termed a "fiduciary". A fiduciary is anyone who at law holds a position of trust and includes executors, trustees, guardians and conservators. Under the UPC the executor is called the "Personal Representative" (the PR).

The PR will submit X's will to the probate court and seek both his appointment as the PR, and the admission of the will to probate. In some states, the proceeding for appointment of the PR will be a formal proceeding involving the need for notice to interested parties and a formal hearing at the probate court. In other states, informal probate without prior notice to interested parties is possible. This allows for the immediate appointment of the PR and later notice to interested parties who may, after the fact, file an objection to the appointment of the PR or the admission of the will to probate.

If there is to be an objection made to the admission of the will to probate or the appointment of the PR, that contest will take place when the will is offered for probate, or within the time allowed for a will contest under the applicable statute of limitations. Grounds for a contest may include a claim of lack of mental capacity, undue influence, insane delusion, fraud, duress, etc.

If there is to be an objection to the court's naming the PR nominated in the will, it will also come at the time the will is offered for probate, or within the period allowed by the applicable statute of limitations. Grounds for objection to the PR can include his lack of capacity, conflict of interest, hostility towards the beneficiaries, etc.

Attention is called to the "applicable statute of limitations" in connection with the discussion above. If there is to be an objection, it is imperative to understand the importance of raising the objection within the period of the applicable statute of limitations.

E. THE IMPORTANCE OF THE APPLICABLE STATUTE OF LIMITATIONS

When individuals come to court to assert conflicting rights, the court is required to decide the dispute put before it. If the dispute concerns a pure matter of law, the judge will decide the case after hearing the arguments put before her by the respective parties - who can appear for themselves (pro se) - or, in the more usual case, by being represented by an attorney. When there are questions of fact in issue, the facts may be decided by a jury, if a jury trial is allowed and if a decision by a jury is asked for.

Being sued for alleged wrongdoing is not something that anyone looks forward to. In order to properly defend herself, a party who is sued will need to spend a good deal of time and money in order to establish a persuasive defense. The law needs to balance the interests of the party who, by right, should be able to seek redress from the court system and the party who is being forced to spend time and money mounting a defense to the charges being made.

It is thought that fairness requires that a time be set beyond which a claim cannot be lodged against a party for an alleged wrongdoing that took place some time ago. It simply seems unfair to allow someone to assert rights that allegedly grew out of events that took place at a remote time in the past. Documents that might have shown a valid defense, or proved that the facts alleged are not true, will be disposed of in time; witnesses will no longer be available, or clearly remember events. There are two major doctrines that allow a party in an action to raise the barrier of time. One is the equitable doctrine of laches, which is a common law doctrine providing that it is unfair to permit a suit after too much time has elapsed.

The other is a statute of limitation, which will be found in an applicable state statute. For a wide variety of actions, the legislature will set a time limit for the period of time in which an action can be brought.

Statutes of limitation can be an absolute barrier against suit. If may seem unfair to prevent someone who has clear evidence of his rights not to be able to bring a wrongdoer to court, but if the applicable statute of limitations has run, and there are no circumstances existing that extend the running of the statute, the party may be unable to successfully prevail in court simply because the applicable statute of limitations has run. The court will not even consider the merits of the case.

The lesson from the above discussion is clear: If there is any objection to a will, or to actions that took place during the life of the party who died, or to any actions taking place during the administration of the estate, prompt action must be taken. This bears repeating: Whenever legal rights are involved, prompt action is necessary.

If a complaint is brought to an attorney, one of the

attorney's first acts will be to check on the application of the applicable statute of limitations in order to be sure that the time for bringing an action has not run out.

F. DUTIES OF THE PR IN CONNECTION WITH THE ADMINISTRATION OF THE ESTATE

Once the will has been admitted to probate, the PR will proceed to marshall the probate assets of the estate, pay the debts and taxes and then prepare to distribute the estate to those who are entitled to receive a share of the estate under the terms of the will.

If there is no valid will, or the will does not dispose of all of the probate assets, the probate property not effectively disposed of will pass by intestacy. Each state has an intestate statute which sets forth the share of the probate estate that will go to the closest relatives if there is no valid will, or the will does not effectively dispose of all of the probate assets. Where there is probate property that is to pass by intestacy, the court will appoint an administrator of the estate for purposes of carrying out the same duties as the PR has in connection with the administration of probate property.

To sum up, for persons without minor children and without substantial estates, who hold the bulk of their property in non-probate form, there may not be a critical need to have even a simple will. Not surprisingly, as wealth increases and as people age, there is a greater need for and use of a will.

If, however, we add to this picture the birth of one or more minor children, we can focus on the need to plan for the possibility of the untimely death of both parents. It is then we can clearly see how having a will can be an essential part of the planning process. For a discussion regarding planning for minor children, see CHAPTER 15.

CHAPTER 14

COMPONENTS OF A SIMPLE WILL

For illustration purposes, let us look at H and W. They have two minor children, X and Y. They have assets held in joint name, insurance, retirement funds and they do not yet have a will.

If H or W dies, the survivor will not have extraordinary problems because there is no will. Their jointly held property will automatically pass to the survivor. The insurance proceeds and retirement funds will pass by the respective beneficiary designations. The survivor will remain as the natural guardian of the person and the property of their minor children. To the extent that there is probate property, under the applicable intestacy statute, it will likely all pass to the surviving spouse, who will become the administrator of the estate. If intestate property is to pass to the minor children, the property will be distributed to the surviving parent as the guardian of the property of the minor children.

Because decedent did not have a substantial estate, there will be no need to deal with the Federal estate and gift tax, and, if there are state transfer taxes, transfers to a surviving spouse may be exempt from that tax, or there may not be enough value to the estate property to trigger that tax. Even if a state death tax is applicable, the rate of that tax will not be great (e.g., 5%).

It is quite unlikely that H and W will die together, or within a very short time of each other, but in rare cases this does happen. The creation of wills by H and W will be helpful in that an organized plan can be created to administer funds available to the minor children in the event of the death of both of their parents.

A. BASIC COMPONENTS OF A SIMPLE WILL

The person who makes a will is referred to as the testator (testatrix for the female). Here are a number of things that the testator can provide for when he executes a simple will:

1. Provision can be made for nominating a personal representative (PR). This can be, and usually will be the surviving spouse. In the event that the surviving spouse fails to qualify or is unable to serve, however, one or more successor PR's can be nominated. The

terms PR and Executor, for our purposes, are two words meaning the same thing - the person, persons or corporate fiduciary nominated in the will to administer the estate. The PR, upon taking office is able to hire an attorney to represent the PR in connection with the administration of the estate. The PR controls the estate administration. For a discussion of who to nominate as PR, see 1-1 below. The guiding principle suggested in these materials for choosing fiduciaries is to pick individuals who you know will be totally trustworthy. Ordinarily, therefore, the fiduciary will be relieved from posting bond.

2. The guardian of the person and property of minor children can be named in order to deal with the possibility that both H and W might die while their children are minors. This will be discussed in 1-2 below.

3. Provision can be made for the payment of debts. This will be discussed in 1-3 below.

4. Provision can be made for the disposition of personal tangible property. This idea is discussed in 1-4 below.

5. Provision can be made for specific bequests. This idea will be discussed in 1-5 below.

6. Provisions can be made for the allocation of the burden to satisfy taxes. This idea will be discussed in 1-6 below.

7. Provision can be made to relieve the PR and other fiduciaries from the necessity of posting a surety bond. For a discussion of surety bonds, see 1-7 below.

8. Provision can be made for defining the "residuary estate". This idea will be discussed in 1-8 below.

9. To the extent allowed by law, fiduciaries can be relieved of the obligation of filing accountings. For a discussion of accountings, see 1-9 below.

10. Fiduciaries can be empowered with a broad range of powers. For a discussion of fiduciary powers, see 1-10 below.

11. A "no contest" provision can be included. See 1-11 for a discussion of this type of clause.

12. The possibility of simultaneous death can be dealt with. For a discussion of simultaneous death, see 1-12 below.

13. The possibility of adopted children, or illegitimate children can be dealt with. For a discussion of this topic, see 1-13 below.

14. The testator's intent regarding the law which she wishes to govern the construction of the will and the implementation of its provisions can be set forth. For a discussion of this topic, see 1-14 below.

15. Provision can be made in the event children are born after the execution of the will. For a discussion of this topic, see 1-15 below.

16. Provision can be made for charitable dispositions. This will be discussed at 1-16 below.

17. A provision can be made to provide for a "pour over" of the residuary estate from the will to the trustee of a living revocable trust. This idea will be discussed at 1-17 below.

18. Trusts can be established to benefit the children. This idea will be discussed in CHAPTER 15.

B. DETAILED DISCUSSION OF ITEMS MENTIONED ABOVE

1-1.   Nomination of a PR

One major idea that should be drawn from this book is that it is extremely important for you to name the right PR in your will. It is equally important for you to name all of the right fiduciaries in your other instruments. A PR need not be the most knowledgeable or experienced person regarding all of the rules in the estate and trust field and the PR need not be close by. But a PR must clearly be honest, have good judgment and have in mind the best interests of those persons who you want to benefit from your estate.

The person who becomes the PR is the person who controls the administration of the estate. The PR hires and can fire professional advisers. The PR often sets his or her own compensation and the compensation of the other professionals. The PR must be absolutely trustworthy. In no case do you want to name a PR who cannot be trusted or who might charge excessive fees for estate administration.

Where all of the estate is to be distributed outright to the surviving spouse, unless there are exceptional circumstances, common sense dictates that the surviving spouse be nominated as the PR. If the estate is to be left to several adult children, consider naming as PR all of the children. This gives all major beneficiaries equal power to make decisions, If then it is deemed practical to have fewer PR, some children can voluntarily decline to serve.

As a general rule, name as PR the persons who will benefit from the will. In that way, those you choose to benefit are able to directly decide what appears to be in their best interest in connection with estate administration. If there are exceptional circumstances, the PR is inexperienced, or does not want to bother with the details of administration, professionals can be named. Importantly, however, compensation will be able to be established by the PR and, if the PR is not satisfied with the work being done, the PR can fire the professionals retained and hire a new group of professionals. Subjecting a loved surviving spouse to another person as PR can be disastrous. CAUTION: If the PR named is an individual, or a group of individuals, circumstances can change. Individuals grow old and may retire, move, lose interest in serving or lose capacity. A corporate fiduciary has the potential of unlimited life. If it does wrong it is subject to suit. Naming a corporate fiduciary as a successor in the event that named individuals fail to qualify or cease to serve is always a good idea. Yet, if a corporate fiduciary is nominated, if the estate is not substantial, minimum fees may cut deeply into the estate.

C. FEES

Fiduciary fees may be based on statutory provisions providing for a fixed percentage which decreases as the size of the estate increases. Or, fees may be reasonable, although it is by no means clear what constitutes a "reasonable fee".

There will be a large group of factors to be considered in determining a reasonable fee if the size of a proposed fee is challenged. But often in a reasonable fee jurisdiction, the PR, or other fiduciary, may charge what he believes the traffic will bear. In any event, it can be quite costly to challenge fees and those costs, when added to the fees, can deeply cut into the size of the estate.

Again, unless the circumstances are truly exceptional, by naming the surviving spouse who is to inherit the entire estate, the testator allows the surviving spouse to be in control. If the surviving spouse predeceases, if the children are old enough and they are to inherit, the children can be named as successors.

Cases of multiple marriages with children from different marriages are complex. Careful planning regarding the nomination of the PR is a must.

1-1. <u>Naming The Guardian</u>

By natural right, a surviving parent is the guardian of the person and property of her minor child. Except in cases where there has been a divorce, or there is a separation or an estrangement, the will's guardianship provision only deals with the nomination of guardian in the event both parents have died and one or more children are minors.

Persons who are under age are not legally able to manage their own property or make decisions regarding their lifestyle. Instead, a guardian of the person of a minor is responsible for deciding upon the proper schooling and living arrangements for the child; a guardian of the property of a minor is responsible for management of the property of the minor.

A guardian of the property of a minor manages that property under the supervision of the appropriate court. Such management can be both inflexible and expensive. Under applicable statute or court rule, the guardian may need advance permission from the court before making discretionary payments on behalf of the minor. Investment vehicles may be limited; expensive formal court accounting, requiring the expense of attorneys

and guardians ad litem may be required. Beyond all
this, at the age of majority (often 18) the guardian of
the property is required to distribute the property to the
minor, whether he is ready to deal with the amount of
property to be distributed or not.

It is because of the harsh rules surrounding
management of funds by the guardian of the property of
a minor that the goal of estate planning, even when
there is a modest estate, is to keep all funds that will be
for minors outside the hands of a guardian. Instead,
those monies will be made payable to the minor's
parent, as an unofficial guardian outside of the court's
control, or, if there are substantial funds involved, the
provisions of the will will call for the distribution of the
minors funds to a trustee of a trust established to
benefit the minor. Again, to avoid undue inflexibility
and expense, that trust will often be set up in a
revocable living trust, so that the funds need not be held
under the direct control of the court (as they would be
if the funds were distributed to the trustee of a
testamentary trust established under the will. Transfer
to a living trust will be discussed in 1-17 below.

1-3.   Payment of Debts

By common law, an executor is responsible for
paying the legal debts of the decedent. By custom,
however, that duty is restated in the will. Furthermore,

the executor may be charged with paying "just" debts, which could include a legal debt which may be non-enforceable in the event that the defense of the statute of limitations is raised. There might also be provision for paying a debt that would otherwise be barred by a discharge in bankruptcy. On the other hand, where the testator does not wish questionable debts to be paid, there may be provision in the will to instruct the executor regarding the testator's intent.

1-4.   Provision For Personal Tangible Property

It is not uncommon for the will to make special provisions for personal tangible property. Personal tangible property includes such items as furniture and furnishings, cars, boats, clothes and jewelry. Where there is a surviving spouse, a clause providing for the distribution of all tangible personal property to the surviving spouse is unlikely to cause difficulty. However, if the surviving spouse fails to survive and the transfer is to be made to the children, complications can arise. If there are minor children, the transfer would be to the guardian of the property of a minor, and that person may not deem it appropriate or practical to save items until the child reaches her majority. Costs of insurance and storage can be unreasonable when the property is not unique and of great value. A provision requiring an equal distribution between the surviving children can bring about disputes about value and right to choose.

In order to reduce the chance for dispute, the will may indicate that the testator may leave instructions to guide the executor in making an equal distribution of tangible personal property. If these informal instructions are to be left with the will, the testator may assign certain properties to certain persons. Since these informal instructions will not be executed with the formalities that may be required for a valid will, the testator may indicate in the will that he hopes these instructions will be followed although he recognizes that they may not have the force of law.

The testator is also free to leave informal instructions to various persons regarding various aspects of the estate administration. Although these instructions may not have the force of the law, they can prove to be extremely useful in moving along the administration and solving various problems that may otherwise come into dispute.

In an extreme case, the will can provide that if issues surrounding personal tangible property cannot be resolved within a certain period of time (e.g., three months) the executor is empowered to simply auction all of the personal tangible property and distribute the proceeds equally among the surviving children.

1-5.   Provision for Specific Bequests

For various reasons, the testator may want to have specific items of tangible personal property bequeathed (property is "bequeathed" by the will; reality is "devised") to named individuals. In drafting a clause for a specific bequest, it is important to clarify intent. Thus, if a gold watch is to be given (the general term "given" can be used instead of the technical legal terms bequeath and devise)to my friend Douglas, it is important to indicate whether Douglas must survive the testator in order to be able to take the watch.

If Douglas predeceases the testator, the will should indicate what happens to the watch.   Perhaps the testator wants the watch to be given to Douglas' son, Franklin, or, perhaps if Douglas predeceases the testator the watch is to be distributed as a part of the residuary estate.

The doctrine of ademption applies to specific bequests. Under the doctrine, if the watch is sold by the testator during his life, the gift of the watch in the will cannot take effect. The gift is adeemed. If the watch is given to Douglas by the testator during his life, the gift is said to have been satisfied.

1-6.   Provision For Satisfying Taxes

The will can allocate tax burdens. Where tax driven

instruments are to be executed, it is most important to pay close attention to the proper allocation of tax burdens. Otherwise, a failure to deal correctly with this issue can result in the bankruptcy of the probate estate (e.g., a large funded revocable trust is established but it is not responsible for any taxes). If taxes are not allocated in the will, local law will control and likely beneficiaries will have a pro rata responsibility for sharing the tax burden.

1-7. Waiver of Surety Bond

The purpose of a surety bond for the PR is to protect against the possibility that the PR will breach his fiduciary duty (e.g., embezzle money, commingle funds, or invest poorly). If the will is silent on the matter of a waiver of bond and there is an individual nominated as PR, the court of probate may require the bond. Normally, a corporate fiduciary is not asked to post a bond because its solvency is regulated by the banking authorities.

If a bond is required, there is a cost involved in gaining the bond, because the surety company issuing the bond is promising to be responsible if the PR breaches her duty and fails to pay back to the estate the monies due from her.

1-8.   Defining and Distributing The Residuary Estate

After all the dispositions discussed above have been dealt with, the remainder of the estate which is referred to as the "residuary estate", is defined by the will. Then the executor is directed to distribute the residuary estate to the persons who the testator wishes to benefit.

The residuary estate can be distributed to one person (e.g., the surviving spouse), or the residuary estate can be divided into the number of shares required to satisfy the provisions of the residuary disposition, and the executor can be directed to make the necessary distributions.

The executor may be required to distribute directly to the named beneficiaries, or, the executor may be directed to distribute a part, or all of the residuary estate, to a trustee of a trust. The trust to be distributed to may be a testamentary trust created by the testator's will, or, a testamentary trust created in someone else's will. Or, the trust to be distributed to may be a living revocable trust established by the testator (perhaps at the same time she executed her will) or established by someone else. When the will requires a distribution of the residuary estate to a living revocable trust (the will referred to as a "pour over will". The idea of the pour over will is discussed at 1-17 below.

1-9.   <u>Waiver of Accountings</u>

As discussed above, formal court accountings can be both expensive and inappropriate in various circumstances. It may be, therefore, that a testator may want to waive the need for such accountings in the will. The difficulty raised by the testator including a provision in the will waiving an accounting is that that provision may not be given effect.

If accounting is mandated by a state statute, or by a court rule, the testator may not have the power to put aside the mandate of the statute, or the court, by making a contrary provision in the will. For that reason, it is not uncommon to find the draftsman of the will providing "to the extent allowed by law, the testator waives the need for accounting ...."

In some cases, a testator may, on balance, want formal court accountings in order to better protect the beneficiaries. Often, however, where one or more long term trusts are to be created, the draftsperson may want to avoid using a testamentary trust provision that creates the trust directly in the will.

The choice of avoiding placing the trust in the will may be determined because of a desire to avoid the need for periodic formal accountings required by applicable state statute. If the trust is set up outside the will, as a revocable living trust, the will can then provide for pouring over the residuary estate to that trust. Unlike the trust set up in the will, the living trust is not under the direct supervision of the probate court, so that neither a statute nor a court rule mandating formal accounting to the court for trusts under wills would be applicable to the living revocable trust.

1-10. Fiduciary Powers

If there is no will and the probate property is to pass in intestacy, the probate court will appoint an administrator to carry out the administration of the estate. In that case, the administrator will have limited powers of investment and this can be quite disadvantageous to the beneficiaries since the opportunity for successful investment during the estate administration can be lost.

Where there is a will, the will can provide the executor with a full set of administrative powers. Customarily, a broad set of powers are provided with the expectation that the executor will prudently choose to exercise powers in an appropriate manner, given the size of the estate and the goals to be accomplished. Estate administration is, by its nature, limited in time. Where there is no Federal estate tax due, it may only take a short time for the executor to marshall the assets, pay the debts (including state death taxes, if any) and prepare to account and distribute. Often the time allowed for creditors to present claims against the estate (e.g., 3-6 months) will determine the length of a simple estate administration.

On the other hand, if a federal estate tax return is due, that return need not be filed for 9 months, and at least that amount of time, or more, may pass before the return is audited and a closing letter is issued by the IRS, thereby ending the Federal estate tax proceedings and positioning the executor to move to accounting and distribution. The trustee of a trust may envision a far longer administration. This, in turn, may make it appropriate to provide the trustee with a broader set of powers than the executor. Often, both fiduciaries are given the same powers but expected to make use of them in a different way. An executor who will be distributing in a matter of months will want to invest differently than a trustee who may be looking forward to a long term administration.

Where a long term trust is being used, it will likely make most sense to name the same parties as both executor and trustee. This will avoid the need for the executor to provide the trustee a detailed accounting and the close of the administration of the estate concerning the executor's stewardship. Coming in as a new appointee, a trustee would be obligated to be concerned with the administration of an executor and would need to see a detailed accounting. This is avoided if the executor and the trustee are the same person. If the trust is to run beyond the normal life span of individuals who could be considered as trustees, it would make more sense to consider the appointment of a corporate fiduciary in order to avoid the need for accounting if an individual were to die in office and a new fiduciary would take over.

a. Statutory Powers vs. Powers Drafted Into the Document

In most jurisdictions, the legislature has created a set of statutory powers for fiduciaries. In some wills and trusts, the draftsman will simply incorporate the statutory powers. Other draftsmen prefer to include in their documents their own set of powers.

Arguments favoring the use of the statutory powers include 1) savings of time and money, 2) not presenting the client with a large number of pages in the document that are unlikely to be read (powers clauses placed in the document can go on for several pages). These pages are referred to as "boiler plate" and are often not closely examined by the client.

Arguments favoring the crafting of powers which are placed into the instrument include: 1) allowing the client to read the provisions he is adopting as his own, 2) allowing the draftsperson to fully craft the powers to the use at hand, and 3) allowing the draftsperson to alter powers as current law affects the field. Certainly, with the advent of the computer, it is much easier to produce large documents at relatively small cost.

If omnibus powers are simply being added to the document to justify a higher charge, there could be justified concern. Further, placing pages of powers into the document should never be done in order to be able to insert in the document truly meaningful and important clauses, such as an exoneration clause or a clause on fiduciary fees, without calling these clauses to the attention of the client.

In any event, if you are presented with a large document, you must be sure to inquire if there is a provision for exoneration and/or fees, or any other special clauses, and, if so, these clauses must be carefully examined and evaluated before the clauses are agreed to. More is said about special clauses in CHAPTER 19.

1-11. "No Contest" Clause

A no contest clause is a special clause which provides an incentive to a beneficiary of the will not to contest the will. An example of such a clause would be: $5,000 to X, provided, however, that X will lose this bequest if he contests my will.

Conflicting policies surround these clauses, since if someone were to be under a wrongdoers influence, the wrongdoer could use the clause to curtail a contest. It is for this reason that a court may read the language of the clause narrowly (e.g., clause limited to starting an action), or, upon a losing court contest, a showing of "good faith" in bringing the action will avoid the effect of the clause.

Unless there is real concern for a contest, this clause is not likely to be seen in your instrument.

1-12. Simultaneous Death

When a person dies simultaneously with someone who is to benefit from her will, or her intestate estate, there is doubt created regarding who the survivor is. Is the beneficiary the survivor? Is the testator the survivor? This matter can be controlled by a clause in the will. In absence of such a clause, where applicable, the matter is dealt with by the Uniform Simultaneous Death Act. Commonly, you may find a clause dealing with simultaneous death in your instrument which will track the provisions of the Act.

1-13. Adopted Persons or Illegitimate

At common law, words such as "issue" or "descendants" were held to exclude adopted persons. Statutes have widely changed the narrow common law construction. Nonetheless, you may find or ask for a clause in your instruments dealing with adoption, particularly if someone in your family has adopted a child. It is not uncommon to find the draftsperson dealing with a matter in the instrument in spite of the fact that underlying law will also bring about the same result.

Depending on your desires regarding illegitimate children, a clause may also be found or asked for in your documents to deal with that issue. Again, statutory law now commonly sets up reasonable default rules if the matter is not spoken of in the instrument.

1-14. Applicable Law

Unless the public policy of a jurisdiction would be offended, the draftsperson can state the law which is to be looked to in the construction and implementation of the instrument. If law is being chosen in order to take away rights from a person, public policy may negate the choice of law written into the document. You may want to discuss this matter with a draftsperson if you have homes in more than one location or plan to move shortly. If you own real property in another jurisdiction, it is important that the property be a non-probate asset in order to avoid the expense and delay of a second, ancillary probate in that other state. Speak to your draftsperson about this matter.

1-15. Afterborn Children

Applicable law may give a share to a child who is not intentionally included in the will. Statutes vary, often applying only to afterborn children. The draftsperson may include language in the instrument to express your intent in order to avoid the application of the statutory provision that would otherwise apply.

1-16   <u>Charitable Dispositions</u>

Commonly individuals may wish to leave bequests to charity. In some cases, the bulk of an estate will be left to charity.

For larger estates, significant tax savings can be achieved through charitable giving. A discussion of the techniques to be used in giving to charity is beyond the scope of this volume.

For smaller estates, and small charitable bequests, it may be more effective for you to informally ask that donations be made by family members after your death outside of the will, in order to avoid the chance that the charitable bequest might complicate the administration of your estate.

If charitable bequests are to be included in your will, consider the following cautionary concerns:

1) Be sure to use the exact legal name of the charity and its exact address. It is most important that there be no room for confusion. A gift simply to "FIRST CHURCH" could result in claims being made by organizations of that name across the

country.

2) If there is a large dollar amount of gift, be sure to remember that for various reasons, your probate estate may shrink prior to your death. A gift of a percentage of the residuary estate, or a share of the residuary estate may make more sense.

3) It is most helpful to include a clause detailing your wishes in the event that the organization you wish to benefit merges with another organization or even closes. Do you want a similar charity to take, or do you want to have the charitable gift not take effect?

1-17. Pouring Over

A will pouring over to a living revocable trust is a common technique used to avoid long term involvement with a court of probate. The reasons for consolidating the estate in a living revocable trust are discussed above. If there is to be a pour over to a living trust, the executor will be instructed in the residuary clause to distribute the residuary estate to the trustee of the living trust so that the funds can be held by the trustee pursuant to the terms of the trust.

1-18 Trusts to Benefit Children.

See the discussion of trust to benefit minors in CHAPTER 15.

Trusts required for children who may be disabled is a far more complex topic that goes beyond the scope of this material.

CHAPTER 15

GIFTING TO MINORS

A. INTRODUCTION

Gifting to minors has been discussed in general terms above. Because of the importance of this issue, this chapter will review the discussion above and provide more details.

Special problems exist where there is a desire to gift property to a minor (or a number of minors). State statutes determine the age of majority, which is often placed at 18 years of age. Minors are under a legal disability. This requires that there be both a guardian of the person and a guardian of the property of a minor. The legal disability of being a minor prevents the minor from administering her own property, (e.g., state law may prevent a minor from buying or selling securities, or entering into a contract). When a transaction needs to be completed for property held in the sole name of a minor, a guardian of the estate of the minor must be appointed so that the guardian can accomplish the transaction. When decisions need to be made as to where the minor will live or go to school, that is the area where the guardian of the person is in charge. Usually, the guardian who is appointed is the parent of the minor (the ward) because the parent is the natural guardian of both the person and property of a ward. If the ward is an orphan, then others need to be appointed.

The difficulty with guardianship is that under state law, it is often an extremely cumbersome management device, particularly with regard to smaller estates. Too often, the expense required to meet state requirements are disproportionate to the size of the estate. This can easily be true if a court must supervise all of the guardian's transactions and give advance approval for all transactions, or the guardian needs to periodically formally account to the court.

In order to lower costs and simplify the management of a minor's property, states have adopted either The Uniform Transfers To Minors Act (UTMA) or its predecessor, The Uniform Gift to Minors Act (UGMA).

UTMA and UGMA authorize trust agreements, the terms of which a donor can adopt simply by having property titled in the name of a custodian holding under the Act. "X, as custodian for Y, the beneficiary" under the UGMA. If assets are titled in this way, X is given all of the flexible powers provided for by the UGMA.

Under the UTMA, a testator, in executing his will, can establish a UTMA custodianship and make a gift to it in the will. By using the device, a testator can easily deal with the possibility that both parents will die, leaving minor children as orphans. While reference to the UTMA allows for a simple solution to this problem, the statute is quite inflexible as compared to a trust provision that can be tailored to a particular situation and then drafted into the will or drafted into a revocable living trust to which the will can pour over. Where provisions are included in the instruments being drafted, in the event both parents die, leaving minor orphaned children, if the assets are to be held by a guardian, each child's assets will be safeguarded until the child reaches the age of majority. Where trust provisions are drafted by the drafting attorney, the assets can be held in trust until the child reaches the age wanted by the individual for whom the instrument is being created.

The disadvantages of UTMA are that: 1) the property held in the UTMA custodianship will be distributed to the child at age 18 and 2) each UTMA custodianship to one beneficiary means that the in the event that there is more than one child, the custodian cannot reallocate property among the decedent's children in response to their changing and varied needs. By using a trust to deal with the possibility of orphaned minor children, much greater flexibility can be achieved.

B. TRUSTS FOR MINORS

A trust for minors can be drawn with the flexibility needed to solve many of the problems that can be thought of in the event of the unlikely demise of both parents while the children are minors. First, the trust can set an age of distribution well above the age of 18.

Next, the creator of the trust, depending on the circumstances, can provide for a lump sum trust allowing the trustee discretion to use so much of the income and principal as necessary to provide for all of the needs of all of the beneficiaries, or the creator of the trust can provide for separate trusts for each beneficiary.

Rather than paying out all of the trusts assets at a specific age, the trust can provide for a staged payout (e.g., 1/3 at age 20, 1/2 of the remaining assets at age 25 and the final payment at age 30).

If desired and allowed in the jurisdiction, the creator of the trust can "spendthrift" the trust, preventing the beneficiary from alienating his interest before it becomes due and preventing creditors from reaching trust assets before they are to be paid to the beneficiary.

During the term of the trust, the trustee can have discretionary power to pay to the beneficiary so much of the income and principal as needed to meet the needs of the beneficiary. If the beneficiary dies before the trust ends, alternate provisions for distribution can be provided for.

While in most cases the planning that can be done to deal with minor children becoming orphaned never actually needs to be used, in the tragic situation where an event does occur, leaving minors orphaned, careful planning in the documents plus the availability of a large insurance policy to cover this unlikely contingency can do a great deal to provide adequate security for minor children who lose both parents. In most cases where the parents are young, the cost of a large insurance policy to benefit the children, if both parents die while the children are minors, will be relatively inexpensive.

For a life insurance policy beneficiary designation, it is important to name a trustee of a trust to benefit minor children rather than to name each minor child. A child would take at majority, whereas a trust can continue until the child's education is completed and the child fully matures.

CHAPTER 16

TAX-DRIVEN ESTATE PLANNING —
THE USE OF A BYPASS TRUST

A. INTRODUCTION

When estate owners have a substantial estate that would be subject to the Federal estate tax, simply leaving the estate outright to the beneficiaries will have death tax consequences on the death of the beneficiaries.

In order to reduce death tax consequences on the death of beneficiaries, planners have learned to take advantage of state property law in order to create a trust - known as a by-pass trust (or also sometimes called a family trust, credit shelter trust or a save the tax trust). We will come to see that judicious use of a by-pass trust together with the use of an optimum marital deduction bequest is the standard estate planning tool to use where one spouse desires the other to receive benefits from a portion of the estate, but wishes to avoid that portion which is in the by-pass trust from being taxed again on the death of the survivor of the spouses.

For simplicity purposes, let us assume that each spouse has one million dollars and we are at the year 2006, when the exemption equivalent available to each spouse is based on the unified credit of 1 million dollars.

If spouse A simply transfers 1 million to spouse B, there will be no tax at spouse A's death. Spouse A's unified credit covers the transfer. However, at spouse B's death, unless spouse B has remarried, the credit available to spouse B will only cover 1 million dollars. Spouse B, unable to employ the marital deduction, will be taxed on the excess 1 million dollars in spouse B's estate.

B. USE OF A BY-PASS TRUST

Use of the by-pass trust can avoid this result.Upon spouse A's death, the million dollars can be placed in a by-pass trust which will simply benefit spouse B, but not be subject to the estate tax on the death of spouse B. Without subjecting the trust property to inclusion in the taxable estate of spouse B, spouse B can be given the right to all of the income from the trust during her life. Although she may not be given a general power of appointment over the property, spouse B may have a right to invade principal for her benefit, so long as that right is limited by an ascertainable standard relating to her support, maintenance, health or education. Such a power, defined as a special or limited power of appointment, does not cause taxation in spouse B's estate.

Spouse B may also be given a so-called "5 and 5 power", the power to invade principal for any purpose (without being limited to an ascertainable standard) as long as the right is limited to the greater of $5,000 or 5% of the principal per calendar year, on a noncumulative basis.

C. THE FIVE AND FIVE POWER

Normally, the lapse (i.e., the failure to exercise) of a power of appointment constitutes a release of the power which, because of the other rights which the spouse has in the trust, will, in turn, cause the released assets to be taxable in her estate. For example, because the spouse is entitled to the income, the release of a portion of the principal will be deemed to be a transfer of such portion of the principal with the income retained by the wife for her life. Ordinarily, that transfer with retained right to income would cause estate taxation. However, the Internal Revenue Code (The Code) provides an exception to this lapse rule.

The lapse of the general power is not treated as a release to the extent that the right to appoint is limited to $5,000 or 5%, whichever amount is greater, of the value of the property during any calendar year, on a noncumulative basis.

Under the "five and five" power, the most that will be included in the spouse's estate will be the value of the unexercised right which she had in the year of her death, because that would not have lapsed. Hence, there will be included in her estate either $5,000 or 5% of the assets in the by-pass trust, whichever amount is greater. All the amounts which had lapsed in the preceding years will not, however, be included in her estate.

D. SPECIAL POWER TO APPOINT TO THIRD PARTIES

In addition to her other powers, the spouse may be given a special power of appointment allowing her to dispose of the assets in the by-pass trust to third parties either during her life or upon her death. The permissible donees may be limited, by the provisions of the trust, to a class such as the couple's children or descendants, or the power may be broad enough literally to permit appointment to anyone to whom the wife may wish to appoint, with the sole exception that she may not be empowered to appoint to herself, her creditors, her estate or the creditors of her estate (power to appoint to that group would create a taxable general power of appointment). So long as the spouse may not appoint to herself, her creditors, her estate or the creditors of her estate, the power will be classified as a special power, rather than a general power of appointment, and hence, the assets subject to the power will not be taxed in her estate.

Giving the spouse the above-described special power adds flexibility to the estate plan and conforms to the concept of giving the spouse the maximum rights over the entire estate. At the time the estate plan is created, the children may be very young. The estate owner cannot know which of the children will turn out to be wealthy, which will turn out to be poor, which will marry well and which will not. The decision of how much to leave to each child, upon the spouse's death, can be left for a later day by giving the spouse this special power of appointment.The spouse, by exercising the power, cannot only designate the portion allocable to each child, but also alter the time or manner in which the children receive the shares. For example, she can effect a change in the trust provisions governing the ages when the children receive their shares free of trust.

E. GREATER FLEXIBILITY CAN BE GAINED BY NAMING AN INDEPENDENT TRUSTEE.

Under certain circumstances, an independent trustee may prove advantageous where more flexible powers are wanted or if a neutral trustee is wanted to insure fair allocation between various beneficiaries.

CHAPTER 17

THE MARITAL DEDUCTION

A. INTRODUCTION

For couples with substantial estates who engage in estate planning, the marital deduction available under the Federal estate tax is an extremely important planning tool.

If a couple sets up their assets in a way that will allow the first to die to fund to the maximum a so called "by-pass trust", then any excess property in the estate of the first spouse to die can pass free of the Federal estate tax, if the property is passed in a manner that will qualify for the marital deduction.

Since its inception in 1948, as a way of roughly equalizing tax benefits in community property and non-community property states, the marital deduction has become unlimited, so that during life and at death one spouse can pass as much property as desired to the other spouse without incurring Federal gift or estate tax.

The theory behind the unlimited marital deduction is that Congress believes that a husband and a wife should be treated as one economic unit for purposes of Federal estate and gift taxes. One major advantage of this theory to married couples is that during their lives there will be no Federal gift or estate tax levied on transfers between the spouses.

To gain the large tax advantage of the marital deduction, certain requirements must be met. Basically, the marital deduction is available only for property passing to a decedent's surviving spouse - and passing in such a way as to be included in the surviving spouse's estate, unless the surviving spouse disposes of the property by spending it or giving it away.

For the majority of married couples in the United States, much of the complication surrounding the use of the marital deduction, can be avoided.

Special rules, for instance, regarding citizenship are inapplicable to married couples who are both citizens of the United States (non citizens, of course, must pay special attention to these rules). Beyond that much of the complications surrounding the marital deductions can be eliminated by giving the marital portion outright, rather than in trust.

NOTE: You do not have to become involved with the complexity and expense of a marital trust unless you decide, after discussing the matter with your planner, that you need to do so.

B. MARITAL TRUSTS

For various reasons, marital deduction trusts are not uncommon. Two such trusts are specifically provided for in The Code and another is sanctioned in the regulations to The Code. In all cases, at the death of the last to die of the spouses, unless the spouse who survived has remarried (and, again, uses the marital deduction) the marital deduction property will be subject to Federal estate taxation in the estate of the spouse who is the last to die.

1. General Power of Appointment Trust

For this trust to qualify for the marital deduction, all the income from the trust must be payable to the surviving spouse and she must be able at her death to appoint the remaining property to a group of people who shall include: herself, her estate, her creditors or the creditors of her estate. It is the fact that the surviving spouse possesses a general power of appointment over the marital assets that will cause the property to be included in her estate at her death.

2. Qualified Terminable Interest Property Trust (QTIP)

With the QTIP trust, the trust creator can name the beneficiaries to take after the death of the spouse. This trust may be particularly helpful to a married person who has children by a previous marriage. It is the required election by the executor on the Federal estate tax return to have the QTIP rules apply to the marital portion that causes the remainder of that portion at the death of the surviving spouse to be taxable in the estate of the surviving spouse.

3. The Estate Trust

This trust, sanctioned by the regulations to the Code, can accumulate income at the discretion of the trustee during the life of the surviving spouse. It is the fact that the remaining marital portion is distributed to the estate of the surviving spouse that causes that property to be included in the estate of the surviving spouse.

C. MARITAL FORMULA CLAUSES

When you sit with an attorney who you have hired to work out your estate plan, if you are married and you have a sizable estate, discussion of the marital deduction will most likely occur. One important matter for discussion is the size of the marital deduction.

One simple way of determining the portion to be

allocated to qualify for the marital deduction is to just pick a figure that at the moment seems close to what the maximum marital portion might be. The obvious disadvantage to this technique is that after the execution of the documents there may be sizable changes of assets, either because of appreciation or depreciation, lifestyle choices or inflation, etc.

Most likely, your legal advisor will want to explain to you that a formula clause will be written into your document for the purpose of defining the marital portion. At that point, there will be a choice made between drafting a marital formula that sets out either a "fractional share" or a "pecuniary amount".

1. Fractional Share

If the marital formula clause speaks of creating a fractional share that will make up the marital portion (e.g., that fractional share of the estate which when taken together with the by-pass trust shall equal the maximum marital deduction needed to avoid the federal estate tax), during the administration of the estate, as the estate appreciates or depreciates the marital portion will increase or decrease reflecting the appreciation or depreciation. Thus, if at the start of administration, the net estate is $2 million, (and the marital share is 1 million) if at the time for distribution the estate has grown to $4 million, the fractional marital share to be distributed will be $2 million; if the estate decreased during administration so that at distribution time the estate was $1 million, then the fractional share marital portion to be distributed will be $500,000.

2. Pecuniary Amount

Unlike a fractional share marital portion, a pecuniary amount marital formula clause will establish a fixed amount at the start of the administration of the estate.

Thus, if at the start of administration the net estate is $2 million and the pecuniary formula marital amount is $1 million, then without regard to the appreciation or depreciation of the estate during administration, the amount of the marital portion to be distributed is $1 million, and a capital gain will be realized by the estate (and a capital gains tax will be payable) to the extent that the marital portion is funded at distribution with assets that appreciated during the administration of the estate. One important advantage is gained by the use of a pecuniary amount formula in the event there is substantial appreciation in the estate during the period of administration. In such a case, all of the appreciation experienced during the course of administration of the estate accrues for the benefit of the persons who are the beneficiaries of the by-pass trust, thereby escaping Federal estate taxation at the death of the surviving spouse. On the other hand, of course, if the estate experiences a significat decline in the value of its property during the course of administration, it is possible that the entire estate will be exhausted in satisfying the spouse's marital portion and no property will remain in the estate to be allocated to the by-pass trust.

C. OUTRIGHT MARITAL DEDUCTION VS. MARITAL DEDUCTION TRUST

The simplest way of qualifying for the marital deduction is by making an outright bequest.

In some cases, however, a marital trust is deemed more appropriate. Examples of when a trust might be wanted include:

1) a spouse who is not interested in, or qualified to manage assets, or

2) a second marriage situation where there are children of a first marriage.

CHAPTER 18

**LOWERING ESTATE VALUES
BY LIFETIME GIFT GIVING**

A. INTRODUCTION

As these materials clearly show, it should be becoming obvious to the reader that if one can lower the value of an estate during life without drawing on the unified credit available to each person, then the estate tax at death can be lowered or eliminated.

For many individuals there is simply not a problem to consider. They do not anticipate having a substantial estate at death. Short of winning the lottery, the tax problems discussed in this book are not relevant. For others, the vast size of their estate makes it imperative that they engage in complex estate and tax planning.

For a sizeable group of individuals who have financial

security and a comfortable lifestyle, the use of one simple technique for lowering the value of an estate can have meaningful results. The technique is consistent gift-giving taking advantage of the annual gift tax exclusion.

Under The Code, each person is able to give up to $10,000 per year to as many different individuals as wanted and so long as the gift is a gift of a "present interest" the gift is totally free of the gift tax. This gift-giving device is separate and apart from the ability to make use of one's unified credit to make taxable gifts during life. Starting in 1999, the $10,000 annual exclusion is indexed for inflation.

B. THE ANNUAL EXCLUSION

Spouses can annually gift for their own funds an amount that is no larger than the annual exclusion. Or, if they so desire, a husband and wife may elect to treat all gifts made by either as having been made one-half by each of them. In this way, they may give up to $20,000 per year to each donee without paying gift tax. Hence, gifts have now become significant planning tools.

The annual exclusion is allowable, however, only for gifts of present, and not future, interest. For an interest to be a present one, the unrestricted right to the immediate use, possession or enjoyment of the asset must be given. The best example of a gift of present interest is an outright gift. However, if a gift is made in trust and the trust provides that the income is to be paid currently to the income beneficiary, the income interest is a present interest, but the gift of principal is a future interest. The value of the income interest is calculated by using a set of tables. Where the trustee is given discretionary powers over the payment of income, or the trust requires that the income be accumulated, there is no gift of a present interest, unless the trust qualified as a minor's trust.

Gifts to persons under age 21 are often desirable. Trusts can also provide income tax advantages when income-producing property is given to a person above the age of fourteen who is in a lower income tax bracket than is the donor. However, since minors (usually persons under age 18) are under a legal disability which restricts the use of property, and since many persons between age 18 and age 20 may not be mature enough to manage their assets, special rules apply to gifts to persons under age 21, which would otherwise be future interest gifts. The Code provides that no part of a gift made in trust to a person under age 21 will be considered a gift of a future interest if the principal and income may be expended for the benefit of such person, and if any amounts not so expended will be distributed to the donee upon reaching the age of 21.

Ordinarily where one pays for the support, medical care or education of a person whom he is not obligated to support, such payments will constitute taxable gifts. For instance, a parent has the duty to support his minor children, but not his adult children. The Code provides for an unlimited gift tax exclusion for amounts paid on behalf of any individual for medical payments or tuition, but not for any other educational or support expenses. Moreover, the payments to be excluded must be paid by the donor directly to the medical care provider or educational institution.

C. FORMULATING A GIFT-GIVING PLAN FOR THOSE WHO CAN AFFORD TO DO SO

Creating a gift-giving program making use of the annual exclusion is a most effective technique for minimizing gift and estate taxes. In formulating the plan, the following matters should be kept in mind:

1. The $10,000 annual gift tax exclusion will, under the provisions of the 1997 Tax Act, be indexed for inflation so that the annual exclusion will be increasing in the future.

2. A gift of a "present interest" must be made in order to take advantage of annual exclusion from the Federal Gift Tax.

3. Property presently given away will immediately be helpful to the persons receiving the gift and those persons will, in the future, gain, if the property is held and it appreciates. The persons given the gift will then be responsible for income taxes on the income earned

by the property.

4. For gifts greater in value than is covered by the annual exclusion, a Federal gift tax return must be filed.

5. If taxable gifts are made, the tax reduces the donor's unified credit. The donor of the gift will not actually be required to pay tax until her unified credit is exhausted.

6. The donor's basis in the gifted property passes to the person receiving the gift (the donee). If the property had been held until the donor's death, his estate would have been able to obtain a stepped up basis in the property.

Example to Illustrate 6.

X needs to decide whether to give a $10,000 in cash, or $10,000 worth of stock in Y corporation. X originally purchased the Y stock for $500 (the purchase price being X's basis in the stock).

If X transfers cash, A's basis in the cash is $10,000. If A spends the cash, there is no income tax consequence. If A receives the stock in Y corporation, his basis will be $500. If he then sells the stock for $10,000, he will have to recognize a gain of $9,500.

If X holds Y stock until his death, his estate will have an increased basis in the stock equal to the value of the stock at X's death (or the alternative valuation date, if that value is chosen to be used in a Federal estate tax return). If Y stock is distributed to A at X's death, A obtains the higher basis in the stock. Because of this basis rule, X may choose not to gift highly appreciated property.

CHAPTER 19

PARTICULARLY TROUBLESOME CLAUSES THAT MAY BE FOUND IN WILLS AND TRUSTS

In this chapter, selected clauses are discussed in more detail in order to alert the reader to the fact that this type of clause may be inserted into a document by a draftsperson. Ideally, the client will be told about the clause and allowed to decide if the clause is wanted. Unfortunately, some draftspersons may simply include the clause. Accordingly, a client should always read the entire document before execution. Asking questions always makes good sense.

A. EXCULPATION CLAUSE

An exoneration clause (also referred to an exculpation clause) is designed to convey the testator's intent to relieve fiduciaries from their normal standard of performance.

By common law, a fiduciary is obligated to use her best efforts to carry out the duties related to her office. Absolute loyalty, an obligation not to co-mingle assets, a duty to properly earmark assets, a duty not to improperly delegate duties and, in general, the highest duty of care is what is expected. In investment the fiduciary must avoid speculations and act in the manner that a prudent man would act.

An exoneration clause may relieve the fiduciary of some of the burdens discussed above. The standard for investment may be lowered. Perhaps the testator has been successful investing in speculations with the person being named executor and the testator would like the executor to continue this type of investment. Suppose the testator wishes to relieve the executor from the standard of prudence in investment because the testator fears that concern for that standard will make the fiduciary too conservative in his approach to investment?

The important thing about an exoneration clause is that it be asked for by a testator. No draftsman should simply place this type of clause in a document without discussing it with the client and determining that this is what the client wanted. Even if the client wants to exonerate the fiduciary, release from responsibility beyond a point may be held to be against public policy and the clause may not be given effect. An example of a provision that might not be upheld is a clause that purported to relieve a fiduciary from liability for intentional negligence.

When an exoneration clause is wanted, it is helpful to indicate (perhaps in a memo left with the will) that the testator wanted the clause and was aware of its inclusion.

B. FEE CLAUSES

Depending on the jurisdiction, fiduciary fees may be set by state statute, or "reasonable" fees may be allowed. Commonly, corporate fiduciaries may have a printed fee schedule. It is important to recognize that unless the corporate fiduciary is willing to bind itself not to change the stated fees in effect when the will is executed (agreements to that effect are rarely made) the corporate fiduciary periodically raises fees.

Testators who are planning to nominate corporate fiduciaries are advised to carefully investigate fees and the philosophy and practices of the corporate fiduciary. Possibly, there is a minimum fee that will be quite high when the amount of assets involved are low. Possibly, if the corporate fiduciary becomes executor or trustee and there are special assets in the estate or trust (e.g., commercial real estate, closed corporation stock) the corporate fiduciary will sell those assets shortly after qualifying and assuming responsibility for administration so that they can organize the assets in a way that will allow them to more easily administer.

When, for various reasons, a corporate fiduciary is wanted (particularly as the primary fiduciary) prudence dictates a conference with the corporate fiduciary who is being considered in order to gain a better understanding of how the fiduciary operates and what actions it would likely take regarding the particular estate being discussed. Other problems that can arise relating to the use of a corporate fiduciary include difficulty if the beneficiaries wish to remove the corporate fiduciary and replace it with another fiduciary.

C. CLARIFICATION THAT EXTRAORDINARY CLAUSE IS WANTED

In order to avoid questions by separate memo, or initials or signature near the extraordinary clause, it can be clearly shown that the person executing the instrument was aware of the extraordinary provision and intentionally wanted it included in her instrument.

CHAPTER 20

GENERATION-SKIPPING DYNASTIC TRUSTS

For a majority of individuals engaging in estate planning, a simple workable plan that will, to the extent possible, protect a surviving spouse and their surviving children is what is needed and wanted. For others with more substantial estates there can be a drive to do more. Protection can be extended to grand-children, now born or to be born thereafter, and later generations. In the states which have now repealed the rule against perpetuities, there is no longer a limitation on the time that property can be held in trust without "vesting". Accordingly, some couples engaging in estate planning will want to create so-called generation skipping transfers that can allow assets to remain in trust in perpetuity, in order to both accomplish death tax savings in the future and also protect all future generations.

Historically, wealthy families would commonly create generation skipping trusts. If X died with a large estate, although he would be subject to the Federal estate tax, he would set up his estate plan so that his surviving spouse, children, grandchildren and later descendants (to the extent allowed by the rule against perpetuities) would on the one hand be able to enjoy the income and principal of the trust (as needed under an ascertainable standard) without there being any Federal estate tax due on the trust assets at the death of the beneficiary. The theory that allowed this windfall is that if the beneficiary is only entitled to the income from the trust during life, at death there is no value to the interest that the beneficiary enjoyed during life. Thus, in successive generations, the trust assets could completely escape estate taxation.

Congress viewed this result as unfairly favoring our most wealthy citizens and, accordingly, it passed CHAPTER 13 of The Code. CHAPTER 13 establishes a generation skipping taxation scheme to tax trust assets held in long term trust so that successive generations are not able to escape estate taxation. The ramifications of the use of generation-skipping trusts today are discussed in the next chapter.

CHAPTER 21

GENERATION SKIPPING TAX

A. INTRODUCTION

For persons of wealth ($1 million plus) a generation skipping transfer trust, taking advantage of the $1 million exemption, may make sense. The most important idea for purposes of this book is to be sure to discuss the subject with your planner.

Historically, individuals with substantial wealth would plan their estates by using a dynastic trusts which could benefit future generations and shelter trust assets from death taxes at later generational levels.

In order to block this obvious unequal treatment favoring our most wealthy citizens, Congress enacted the generation-skipping tax ("GST") in 1986.

$1 Million Exemption

On the one hand the GST blocks the sheltering of assets from the estate tax by creating a complex system for taxing estates where the decedent had access to funds from earlier generations. More importantly, however, the GST preserves limited planning using a generation-skipping trust because under the GST each individual transferor has a $1 million exemption from the GST that may be allocated by the transferor or the personal representative of the transferor to any lifetime or testamentary transfer made.

The $1 million exemption from the GST may be allocated at any time on or before the date for filing an estate tax return for the transferor. The portion of any trust to which the exemption is allocated will be sheltered from the GST and, to that extent, the trust can operate as a classic generation-skipping trust, sheltering future generations from estate tax while allowing those beneficiaries to enjoy trust benefits without being subject to the estate tax or the GST at their death.

Grandfathered Trusts

Generation-skipping trusts created years ago are grandfathered from the GST tax. Grandfathered trusts include: 1) irrevocable trusts created on or before September 25, 1985, and 2) revocable trusts or trusts under wills executed prior to October 22, 1986, and not amended thereafter, as long as the grantor or testator died before 1987, and 3) certain other previously created trusts.

For any trust previously created, be sure to check with your planner before carrying out any plans regarding a previously created trust.

Uses of Exemption During Life

If a lifetime trust is being created and if there is a likelihood that property placed into the trust will appreciate, it may be desirable to allocate all or part of an individual's GST exemption to the trust. By allocating the exemption early to a lifetime trust, all of the appreciation of the trust's principal will be sheltered from the GST. Thus, once a trust is established to take advantage of the $1 million exemption, future appreciation in trust property is sheltered. In a case where this planning device is to be considered, the importance of accurate valuation must be seen. Ideally, one does not wish to risk filing a gift tax return showing an early allocation of the exemption, and then risk a subsequent reevaluation by the IRS which could cause the value of the property to exceed the exemption allocated to it, with the result that the transferred property would be only partially "exempt" from the GST.

Married Couples

With married couples, the arrangement of assets in a way that permits each spouse to use his or her exemption is important.

With respect to gifts during lifetime, married couples should generally make split gifts of property interests that have generation-skipping tax potential so that all or part of each spouse's exemption can be allocated to one half of the gift. If the exemption is not completely used during lifetime, the estates of the married couple can be structured to most effectively utilize the exemption of each spouse. A planner experienced with the GST can deal with the complex planning required to accomplish this.

Charitable Split-Interest Trusts

Where a charitable objective is being combined with the opportunity to take advantage of the $1 million GST exemption, special rules apply. Again, it is most important to work with a planner who is totally familiar with the GST, if the exemption is to be most effectively used.

CHAPTER 22

RECAPITULATION

If you have come this far in the book, you have discovered several things:

1) Estate planning is a complex subject.

2) Most likely you will need the help of a competent lawyer.

3) In creating a plan, you need to focus on the unique situation that you and your family are in.

4) Whenever possible, it is best to choose a simple plan.

5) Whenever possible, it is best to keep control within your own family.

6) You must always be careful to understand what you are signing and what you are planning to do.

7) Periodically, as your circumstances change, you must review and modify your plan.

As was stated at the start of this book, the object of the book is not to turn you into an expert in estate planning or to answer every question that may come up.

If the book has given you a broad overview of the field and made you sensitive to the obvious pitfalls to be avoided, then the book has indeed accomplished what its author intended it to do.